D1269113

Origins of Art

THE GOND VILLAGE OF PATANGARH

KODAI MATSUOKA   **t**   BHAJJU SHYAM

Tara Books

 Bhajju Shyam belongs to a section of the Gond community called the Pardhan Gonds. Traditionally, the Pardhans were the bards and storytellers — today, many of them are renowned artists, who have given visual form to the traditional myths and beliefs of the community.

We've known Bhajju for over 15 years, and collaborated with him on a variety of book projects. We became close friends during the time we worked together on the now iconic *The London Jungle Book* — and brainstormed on how to turn his experience into a visual travelogue. At that time and later, one question kept coming up: how was Bhajju to render his own individual experience, in his own way, while staying within the community style of painting that he had inherited? It was a genuine struggle for him. But in the end, it was resolved masterfully in the book.

Over the years, with Bhajju, we found ourselves coming back to this question: how is an artist to take a tradition forward, while remaining rooted to its essence? To this day, the question remains important for Bhajju, as he continues his committed and passionate search for answers.

Bhajju is based in the city of Bhopal, but considers the village of Patangarh, where he was born and brought up, as central to this quest. Not just in a nostalgic sense, but as a physical and cultural location which gave birth to what is popularly known as Gond art, but is actually practised by a particular community called the Pardhan Gonds. In many ways, he embodies in himself and in his work the knowledge and traditions he grew up with. But he is also aware that there is much more to discover — and much of it is dying out — so he is curious, and deeply invested in preserving what he can of this heritage. On his frequent visits to Patangarh, he talks to village elders about tree lore, how they classify soil or forecast rain; he gathers forgotten oral stories from the few old storytellers still around; he organises workshops for women who create decorative floor and wall designs; he invites the 'bhujrukhs' — travelling bards — to perform in his ancestral home... we discovered all this, and more, through our conversations with Bhajju.

We also explored many of these themes and ideas in the books we created with him and other artists. And, for all of them, Patangarh — and the forest that surrounds it — remains central to their collective memory, feeding their art and imagination. We have been well aware of this link not just from what the artists told us, but from our visits to Patangarh. The subject fascinated us, and we were keen to explore the connections between art, imagination and lived life in depth, if the right opportunity presented itself.

From our work with the Pardhan Gonds (and other indigenous artists in India) we knew that this was an important challenge, but we also realised that we still had a long way before we could formulate a theory of art created by artists, and practised by "ordinary people" living in different rural communities across India.

We had meanwhile formulated a set of questions that appeared important: how did these practices originate and grow? What role did place, nature, culture and individuals play? Were there extraordinary people who could change the course of tradition into a radically different direction? What did supportive social and aesthetic interventions from outside, by individuals and institutions, offer artists? Through research and conversation, we had arrived at some answers, but on the whole, our knowledge remained fairly abstract and anecdotal. We needed a founded, empirical starting point, a tangible focus from which we could begin to map out these connections.

It came to us in a wholly unexpected and serendipitous fashion. In 2017, there was a retrospective of our work, an exhibition curated by the Itabashi Art Museum in Tokyo, Japan. One of the exhibits focused on our classic title *The Night Life of Trees*, featuring three well-known Pardhan Gond artists, including Bhajju Shyam. The display of original art was cleverly interspersed with stunning photographs of the village of Patangarh, taken by the Japanese photographer Kodai Matsuoka. We knew his work from earlier, and were aware that his passion for Gond art had taken him to Patangarh. But the impact that his images made on us — in large format and juxtaposed with original paintings — was powerful. It set us thinking once more about the connections between life worlds and art practice — and we wondered what Bhajju would have to say about these photographs.

In that instant this book was born, as we asked ourselves: why not have Bhajju comment on Kodai's pictures, and tease out the meanings that only he could bring to them? We could present him with a set of images from Patangarh, based on themes that he himself had brought up earlier, as points of reference while thinking about the origins of Pardhan Gond art. Kodai was delighted to take this mission on. He re-visited Patangarh, this time accompanied by Bhajju, and took a whole new set of pictures. Once these images were in, we invited them both to an extended conversation with us, around the photographs. What emerged from this encounter was more enriching than any of us could have imagined.

While designing the book, we decided to include appropriate illustrations by the Pardhan Gond artists we work with, to offset the photographs. We didn't ask them to create images specifically for this book, but decided to pick out appropriate illustrations from already published work. During the process, we noticed how uncannily accurate these images were, in relation to the photographs, even though they were not rendered in a "realistic" style. This was a revelation. We've tried to bring all these threads together in a narrative form that lays some of the foundation stones — in a lived sense — of how art arises and grows.

Gita Wolf

Kodai Matsuoka

Many years ago, at a bookstore in Delhi, I came across a book called *The Night Life of Trees.*

It was a magical book, with paintings and tree lore by three artists from the Gond tribe in Madhya Pradesh.

I was so moved by that book that I immediately wanted to follow its trail, which led me to one of the artists, Bhajju Shyam and to the small village of Patangarh, where he was born and brought up.

It turned out that the other two artists from the book — Ramsingh Urveti and Durga Bai — also came from Patangarh. A village which nurtures such beautiful art, I thought, must be a very special place. I discovered later that the great master of Gond art, the pioneering Jangarh Singh Shyam, also came from Patangarh.

Now I had no doubt that I needed to go to Patangarh myself, to the birthplace of this incredible art. I was particularly fortunate that Bhajju agreed to take me around.

I'm a photographer, and that is my way of recording my experience. But as this project developed, we realised that I need to say more with words, and that Bhajju's comments on my photographs would be important too. So this book has turned out to be a dialogue between the two of us, on Patangarh.

But first, I need to begin my journey with a homage to *The Night Life of Trees.*

Bhajju Shyam
The Home of the Creator
from The Night Life of Trees

Ramsingh Urveti
The Night of the Glowing Sembar
from The Night Life of Trees

Durga Bai
The Dumar Tree
from The Night Life of Trees

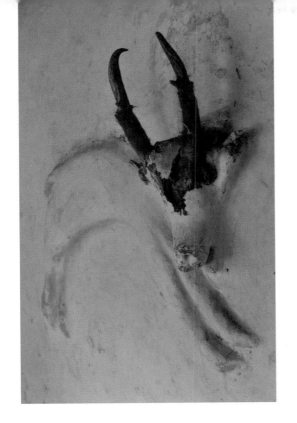

There is a brightness that is particular to Patangarh. Maybe because of its location — the village sits on top of a hill and is filled with sunshine.

As Bhajju and I walked around, I began to think about the late Jangarh Singh Shyam and what he brought into the village, and what he took from it. He moved to Bhopal as a young man, and began experimenting with a new way of painting. He is the one credited with putting Gond art on the course it is on now.

From what I understand, he took the rich decorative and mural techniques of the village to a new level and began making paintings of Gond stories. Sadly, Jangarh died far too early under tragic circumstances in Japan. But I can see how much wealth he brought culturally and economically to Patangarh.

This is not to say that Patangarh is an exceptionally rich village — it's just that there's a richness to life here that is beyond the material. Perhaps this is because of the art that is evident everywhere.

Jangarh Singh Shyam
Deer
from Beasts of India

Being with Bhajju in Patangarh allowed
me to see things and meet people that
I never would have, otherwise.

As a foreign visitor, I tend to be nostalgic,
longing for what we've lost in our culture
in Japan. These vanished art forms survive
at best in museums, frozen in time. A lot of
the images and symbols in Bhajju's art and
in Gond mythology remind me of Japanese
customs and characters that have disappeared.
I worry about this loss of culture and history.

Maybe that's what led me to chronicle
Patangarh's unique history, particularly
its art-making. Even though it changes and
evolves all the time, art remains an archive
of the past — it has the power to find order
in chaos, to retain what is enduringly present,
while adapting to the new in other ways.

Bhajju Shyam

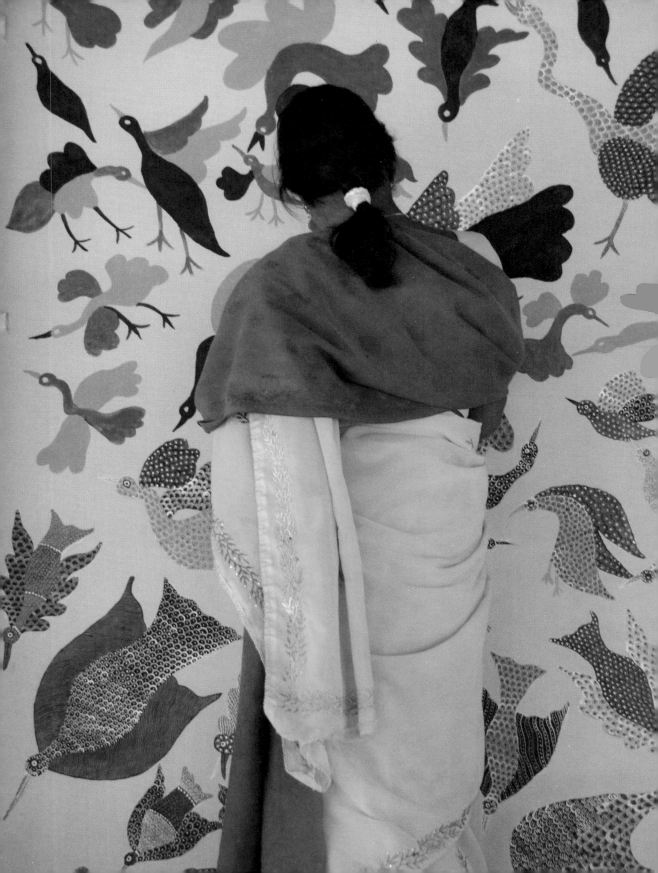

Patan — that's what we call Patangarh — is a happy place. There's always something or the other happening here… rituals, dance, song, festivals. We love any kind of celebration! Over the last few decades, it's also become a bit of a tourist destination.

I first met Kodai when he came to Patangarh — like so many others — to learn more about the place, and about Gond art. There have been many researchers who have come before him, so I assumed that he'd spread the word — like the others did — about our culture and history.

When we went around the village together, I had no idea then that it would end up as this book, which has become a conversation on Patangarh between Kodai and myself.

Patan was well-known, throughout history, for different reasons. Our deity, Thakur Dev is said to reside here. The famous anthropologist Dr. Verrier Elwin made it his home, and settled here after he married a Gond woman. But it was my uncle, Jangarh *Chacha*, who was most influential for the future of Patangarh and Gond art. When he started out, not a lot of people knew what Gond art was. But in the last decade or so, everyone seems to have heard of it. Jangarh Chacha was the one who made it famous.

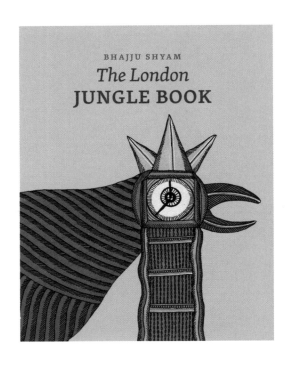

As for me, maybe more people found out about me and Gond art after *The London Jungle Book* came out. Many years ago, I went to London to paint murals on the walls of a restaurant, and this book was about my experiences there.

In 2018, I was honoured with a prestigious national prize for art, the Padma Shri Award. As more people came to know about me, they also came to know of my village, Patangarh. And not just the village either, even the district it's located in! In fact, news of my award seemed to have reached places before I did. On my way to Patangarh after the award was announced — we'd stopped at a railway crossing — a few local journalists suddenly swooped in out of nowhere and started interviewing me. Everyone was so proud of the fact that this was the first time a Gond artist had won the Padma Shri.

I think Jangarh Chacha would have been really happy to see all this today. He was the one who started it all, and for him to see how the art form has grown, the recognition it has won, would have been very special.

I keep hearing that with some other art forms, there is dwindling interest, or that the form is stagnating, but I only hear positive things about where Gond art is headed: it continues to flourish.

Bhajju Shyam
Working for the Stomach
from The London Jungle Book

I think of this book as a blessing,
not just for me, but for our whole village.
With *The London Jungle Book*, I could only tell
my own story, my journey through my eyes.
But with this book, I can introduce people
to Gond culture and Patan's history — I'm
thankful to be doing this along with Kodai.

He tells me that he wants to archive and
nurture art traditions — that's a very moving
thought. It is only the most passionate who
can take on this kind of work. I see this
book as a way of ensuring that our history
is not forgotten, it will leave something
behind for the coming generations.

And it's not just about our art, but also about
the other forms of celebration and community
— which feed our art. I worry that we're also
losing our language, and the minute it's gone
entirely, we lose our history and culture.

Kodai has travelled so far for a project that's
not even about his country. And I find myself
thinking about how *The London Jungle Book*
captured my experience of a different culture...
this book is doing the same for Kodai.
I think this is Kodai's own "Jungle Book"!

Contents

Life · Time

Kodai (K): In the years that had passed since my first visit to Patangarh, what surprised me the most when I went back was how quickly the infrastructure had grown. Roads are now paved with asphalt and many houses have electricity.

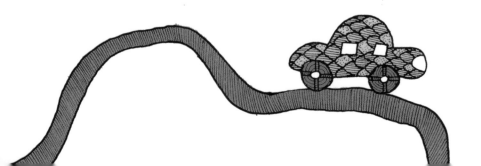

Bhajju (B): A lot has changed in Patan. I notice this each time I return from Bhopal, where I live now. To me, Patan is not as poor as it once was. I remember how it used to be a big thing for someone to have a TV in their house in the old days: we would all go to that person's house to watch a show or even just to look at their TV! But TVs are not really that expensive now, and many people can afford to buy one for their own household.

B: It really was different when I was growing up. Back then, our lives and livelihoods were completely dependent on rain and a farmer's income would rely entirely on the harvest. He would put in blood, sweat and tears in the hope of a good yield.

Even now, most people carry on the work of farming as they used to, with the old implements and tools. A farmer's day still goes on as it always did. Girls continue to bring food cooked by womenfolk for their families working in the fields.

But some things have changed. Farmers in Patan feel they can tide over the situation, even if they have a poor crop yield. Since the village council for the area is based in our village, we get to know of other work opportunities. Also, today, people are more ready to go to the city and take up some manual labour to survive, if they have to.

The important thing is that the city is no longer far away, since the roads are better. We now have frequent buses that take us to the city. So both men and women are ready to take on multiple jobs these days.

We also have mobile phones now and so we feel more connected to the city.

There have also been some government initiatives over the years to better our lives, and among other things, food staples have been heavily subsidised. No one really goes hungry in the way they did earlier.

But if you step outside Patan, there's no denying that the old problems still exist: there's hunger, lack of water, worry over crops — and you wonder if it is viable at all to be a farmer anymore.

K: One thing hasn't changed in Patan — there's no piped water in the village yet. It's still a woman's chore to walk all the way down the hill to the well in the morning, to fill pots with water that the whole family will use through the day.

B: Traditionally, the men work in the fields and take their cattle out to graze. And it's women who go to collect water. Of course, there's no reason why only women have to fetch water, but that's the way it has always been, and it continues to this day. It's usually the first thing they need to do when they wake up.

K: If there was a water connection in the village, it would bring in drastic changes to village life. Women would be free from these chores and perhaps have more time during the day. When I was taking these photographs, I found the way in which women balanced the water pots on their head so beautiful. But then, I reflected, that for a foreign visitor, it is easy to say "beautiful", while the actual chore might be the toughest part of their day for these women.

Then again, I realised that a village well is not only a place that supplies water, but it is also a spot where women can socialise, safe for a period from prying eyes and the constant responsibility of family. It used to be that way, in Japan.

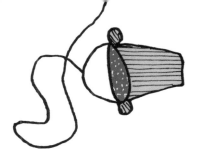

B: Things have changed a bit with the water situation. I remember when women would have to walk nearly two kilometers to the Narmada or Shivri rivers, to the water source. But now we have water tanks in the village. Back then the tension was about finding water, now it is about your turn in the water queue, and how you will manage to carry your pot back!

There are also small wells that farmers have dug next to their fields. The water is meant for their crops, but they don't mind people from the village drawing water to drink from these wells — so we do help each other out in Patan.

We still need to be very careful about how we use water. We use it wantonly in the city — litres of water for every bath — but here in Patan you bathe using one bucket of water. And you also learn to divide up the water you have into what you need it for — this much for drinking, this much for cooking, and the rest for guests or washing up.

B: So what really makes Patangarh unique? When I think it over carefully, I feel that the biggest factor is art. Gond painting has become renowned in the last few years.

It's a cultural asset, but it's also commercially important. Almost every family is likely to have an artist — someone who has most likely moved to Bhopal. Of course, not everyone can build a stable career out of painting, and not everyone can move to the city.

Only people with the means, and the right family connections, can afford to live in Bhopal. But then interestingly, even people who have stayed behind in Patan have started painting seriously.

Meanwhile, they also continue to farm and employ *adivasis* from other villages to help them out!

Bhajju Shyam
The Birth of Art
from Creation

Earth · Life

Kodai (K): Walking around one afternoon, I came across a girl carrying something large on her head — it was a parcel wrapped in cloth. She said she was taking lunch for her family who were working on their farm. I asked if I could come along, and she didn't seem to mind. She stayed firmly on course, not even stopping to chat with a few women around the well, who called cheerfully out to her.

K: As we came to their field, her father spotted her right away... lunch!
The whole family gathered under the shade of a tree, and unpacked the lunchbox.
The father was the one who was served first, and then all the others followed.

It was a lovely pastoral scene, reminding me of all the times I ate outdoors with my family — though my father was a location surveyor, not a farmer.

Bhajju (B): It's hard work on a farm, and people usually work all day. It's the women who bring them lunch. Sometimes a child might be asked to do this — especially when it's a school holiday or over the weekend; or perhaps the older women in the household are out of the house, or maybe working in the fields too. It's unusual now, though, for children to bring lunch. But they do sometimes, and the child might even have cooked it herself.

It's the men who are fed first, whether in the field or at home. There's usually one woman who's serving everyone else, both men and women. Even in homes where everyone eats together, there's usually someone serving the meal.

Farm workers also love to drink 'pej' — a kind of watery gruel made from rice and millets. It's very filling and nutritious, particularly for people who work hard in the fields all days. No child would be entrusted with carrying pej though — it might spill. It's usually an older woman who carries it carefully to the fields.

B: Most farmers in our village own their own land. But these plots tend to be fairly small, from about half an acre to two acres. They are also this tiny because land usually gets divided among family members over generations. People also lease land from others who can't afford to keep it going. We call this 'adhiya'. Not all land is suitable for cultivation though. Gond thought, in fact, divides the earth into seven types, from fertile and riverine to rocky and forested.

There are no tube-wells or irrigation channels in Patangarh. Farming here runs on sheer faith in the clouds above. Whatever rains down on a field is all a field will get. You can imagine what that's like during bad monsoon years. But it is not as though farmers are ignorant or that they are not aware of seasonal rhythms. When the red caterpillar emerges out of the earth, they know it is time to start sowing seeds. Or when swarms of a particular insect called 'battar' emerge suddenly, the rainy season is about to begin.

Bhajju Shyam
Seven Types of Soil
from Creation

B: Traditional farming wisdom also requires that we put aside cobs of corn into 'storage' on a kitchen shelf, on no account to be eaten or touched. We call this 'bijha', and it's meant for good luck, to ward off the evil eye, and ensure prosperity. Because it's in the kitchen, visitors can't spot it, and the householders would rather die of hunger than touch that corn, even in times of drought or extreme poverty. It is that sacred.

Wheat was always our main crop, with some rice, but ever since soya beans were introduced, lots of farmers have taken to it — there's more money in it. It's also much tougher to grow wheat, though there are still people who work at it. We don't actually eat soya beans, it's a cash crop to get a bit of money. You can buy a new dress for a child, or even a piece of jewellery, if things go well.

Then there are the various beans, lentils and seeds which, traditionally, we grew for oil or for their medicinal properties. We grow vegetables too, but these are seasonal, and dependent on the rains. Nowadays it's more common to buy vegetables in the market than it used to be. The market is closer now, and it's good for getting in onions or potatoes.

Generally, we cook what we grow. 'Sada-bahar' — just greens — grow freely all year around. We cook them fairly simply and eat them with locally grown rice, which is short and sticky, not like the fine refined rice in the market. Add to this some fiery little green chillies and some *dal*, and you have a typical meal. On special occasions there could be small local river fish, or produce from the market. Most people tend to eat a mix of what they grow and what they can buy.

B: But living in a farming community isn't just about growing food. Being outdoors, especially as children, means that you get to know all kinds of plants, some of which have no real "use". We used to play "cars" with the pods from a really thorny plant as children, running them back and forth to make a whirring sound. Children playing pretend would find ways to insert these thorny pods (combined with other seeds) into the heels of shoes and the "chrrrrr chrrrr chrrr" noise they made signalled that the wearer was someone important in the village — maybe a rich person, or the village head. They'd call it the 'bajne wala joota' or musical shoes. A bit like the squeaky shoes that children wear these days.

Apart from play and the joy of being out in the open, as children we would look forward to the many festivals and celebrations which came around regularly. It was just part of life, but now, as an adult, I think more about the meanings of these occasions.

For instance, we celebrate the sowing season with a "seedling" festival, when girls pray to a pot of sprouting grain, for nine days, and there is singing and dancing all night. Finally, on the tenth day, the sprouting seeds are scattered into the soil and watered.

It's a ceremony to give thanks to the miracle of food and new growth, which allows us all to live. So our rituals, ceremonies and stories are connected to the land, to nature, and to our lives in a deeper way. Gond stories of creation are about this connection.

K: It seems to me that farming, for the Gonds, is not merely about growing food: it is linked to the life they lead, and in a sense, to larger belief systems.

Even the age-old tools they use have evocative names and stories attached to them. I was drawn to the ploughing tools and the threshing process, in which bulls circle around, threshing the harvested grain. Apart from their function, the tools were beautiful objects.

B: There are two kinds of ploughs on our farms — the everyday one, and the special one we call the 'naari', which means woman. You put seeds through one end of the naari. Two people are needed to work it, as it ploughs and sows at the same time. One of them is usually the farmer who's harvesting the grain. Many people do use tractors now, but there are still some who use the naari because they can't afford a tractor, or simply prefer the old way, which they say works better.

This is not to say that everything new is bad. Take the old way of separating chaff from grain: they would lift the basket high up and toss the grain in the air, letting the wind blow out the chaff. The fallen grain had to be then separated and gathered by hand. It was hard work. But now people use a sieve, which is easier and faster.

But thinking in a broad way, there is something valuable in a lot of the old ways, which I would call a particular relationship to the land and the work of farming. It's not a mechanical extraction of food, dumping stuff on the earth without caring how she's fed. There is observation, care and craft involved.

Take the tools, for example. The naari is a beautiful tool made by special craftspeople who carve it with great care. And the people who use the naari also take careful pleasure in the act of ploughing.

K: It occurs to me that once upon a time, people in Japan must have farmed like the Gonds did. We still have festivals for fertility and a good harvest, in spring and autumn. But we seem to celebrate them without knowing what the festivals are for. We don't recognise that farming is involved because most of us no longer have that knowledge and connection to the earth anymore.

Life · Home

Kodai (K): Since my first visit to Patangarh, I have noticed a major change and that has to do with people's homes. The old homes made with traditional materials are being replaced with concrete houses, at a very rapid rate.

Bhajju (B): I wish we could keep our traditional houses the way they used to be. But it's difficult, in today's times. The problem now is: where are the materials? How do we build these houses? The same government initiatives that helped subsidise basic food items have also encouraged the building of new concrete, brick-and-mortar houses. There are very few traditional mud houses left now.

K: Whenever I visited a traditional home in Patan, I would be welcomed and seated in the *aangan* or courtyard. The decorated courtyard was the open space, as soon as you come in through the outer door. The actual rooms of the house surround this area, so the courtyard was in between public and private, inside and outside. As a space it is crucial for the way social life is conducted in the village, especially for the women.

B: The courtyard was the most important aspect of a traditional house. It is really where everything happens in village life — the floor is painted, visitors (including animals) are welcomed, celebrations are held...

K: I worry that the layout of the new houses, which look like standard concrete blocks, changes the nature of community interaction.

But I also know that tradition is something that changes… it cannot be a legacy that is stuck in the past. Bhajju also tells me that it is getting more and more difficult to source original material for building traditional houses — wood, tiles, rope, mud.

B: There are so many aspects to traditional homes which are connected to how life and art come together in the village: the walls, the aangan, the granary and even shelves would all be decorated with reliefs and paintings.

B: The most important aspects of a traditional
home are the courtyard and the granary.
The courtyard connects the home to the outside
world, and the granary acts as the store of the
family's wealth. People store not just grain,
but most things they value in their granary.

Rajendra Kumar Shyam
Granary
from Between Memory and Museum:
A Dialogue with Folk and Tribal Artists

B: It is getting harder and difficult to build houses in the traditional way. More and more trees are being cut, so there are no forests left to gather traditional materials, as we used to. Take bamboo or wood... you have to go at least fifty kilometers, deep into the forest, and it's both illegal and risky. Then you need a vehicle and the costs add up. Some people feel it's just not worth it.

Take something like tiles: traditional tiles need repair or replacement every year, and people would labour over it every summer. So when someone builds a new concrete house, if the family wants a tiled roof, they prefer buying tiles that don't require so much upkeep. You can easily tell the tiles apart: the commercial ones are different, less individual. The old houses may look imperfect, but they have more character. Some people in the village, very few, still choose to work at the old tiles, in spite of the difficulty in getting old materials.

B: Nowadays, it's mostly farmers with many family members still living in the village who have the old, traditional houses. Those who can lay their own bricks and build their homes from scratch. The sand you find in our village is particularly strong, but it's a long and laborious process to bake mud bricks — sometimes it takes months. There are also people who build walls with regular bricks but plaster it with mud instead of cement. A modern house made to look traditional!

We used to have a system called 'bigaar' which was common. You would invite your family and friends to come and help you — to build or repair a house, or help in the farm when extra hands were needed — in exchange for food, and maybe a place to stay if they were from another village. No money was involved. So everyone pitches in when you need them, and you return the favour when they call you. It's still around, this system, but much less now.

Apart from the changes in labour and materials, there is one main problem, as I see it, when the old changes into the new... no one has given a thought to how the new houses are designed. You can sleep on the floor in the old houses because it's not as hard as concrete, granite or marble. The tiles are designed to let cool air through. The kitchens are not hot and airless... none of this seems to have been considered when people build concrete houses. To me, the greatest shortcoming with the new houses is that they have no courtyard. Every bit of space seems to go into building rooms like shoe boxes, stacked onto each other.

B: There are a few people who have tried to innovate and compromise when they want to renovate an old house. My brother, for example, rebuilt his house, but he kept the courtyard. He just broke down the mud walls of the old house and put up brick and mortar walls in their place. There's no wood or bamboo to repair his house even if he wanted to go the traditional way. But the courtyard will stay. I think we all decided that this would be the way to honour our ancestral land and the home we inherited.

It's not a bad trend — there is a lot of rebuilding going on, and people have seen what we've done. A few people have tried to retain the courtyard, when they build a new house. It's better than nothing, but we don't seem to have the time and thought to arrive at the kind of design which was there in the old houses. We think about how to carry the good parts of traditional housing forward, keeping in mind modern needs and the availability of material. We need ideas, and time and work to carry them through.

So, what can we do? It looks like you have to be really well-off to maintain old traditional houses, or renovate them in a way that the good parts of tradition are kept alive despite modern constraints. It's strange but true.

Life ▪ Trees

Kodai (K): I was led to Patangarh by the book called *The Night Life of Trees*, in which Gond artists painted their stories of trees, especially tales of the forest spirits and gods which exist within them. Bhajju was one of the artists in that book. When I got to the village this time, I realised why Gond artists were so inspired... Patan had some of the most magnificent trees I have ever seen.

Bhajju (B): Amongst all the trees, if there is one that is central to Patangarh's identity, it would be the Patan tree. Everyone in the area knows this ancient tree, which people say has been around for centuries. It's believed that the god Thakur Dev lives in it. He rules in his world — called 'Dev Raj' — which is under the ground. Which is why our village is called 'Patan-garh' — the bastion of the gods. The 'garh' in Patangarh stands for 'bastion.'

K: For me, it was very easy to connect to these ideas because we have a similar culture in Japan. There are huge old trees in village shrines in Japan where people often go to pray. These trees are called 'shinboku' in Japanese, meaning god's tree. And regardless of religion, we all believe that trees have spirits.

B: We have a close relationship to trees in Patangarh, also in a more everyday sense. Some of them play a role in particular rituals or festivals, others are connected to food or medicine, and some just provide shade and a place to play.

The Semar tree is central to Holi festivities. Its twigs are twisted together like rope, and people poke each other in the stomach with it. It's supposed to have medicinal properties, they say it cures digestive problems.

There are trees which are always full of
honeycombs. I even remember seeing
them as a child. I would watch a bird fly
around the honeycomb, picking at it…
the bees got really angry! They would start
buzzing around, and we would end up
running for our lives around the village,
chased by bees! My children don't have this
kind of knowledge or experience, growing
up in the city. Only kids who still live in
the village do and when you grow up with
that kind of learning, you retain it for life.

79

B: I would say that our connection to trees is formed by playing close attention to the rhythms of nature. For instance, we eat the delicate budding leaves of the Pakri tree. The thing is, this leaf is edible only during a few hours on a particular day — if you miss it, that's it, it becomes tough and starts to taste bitter. You can only tell which day that would be by keeping a close watch on the tree. After it has shed all its leaves and is barren for a few days, you will see tiny little buds one day.

When they appear, you know that the leaves are getting ready to sprout by the next morning. And that's the one day the new leaves are tender enough to be eaten.

People crowd around the tree early in the morning, ready to pick them. And every so often, someone gets told off for breaking the branches, instead of plucking just the new leaves. This minute attention to time and the rhythms of nature forms the basis of our relationship to trees.

B: The everyday connection we have with trees has given rise to a profound Gond belief: that trees are really busy during the day, giving humans and other creatures food, shelter, and medicine. So it is only at night, when their work is done, that they relax, and allow the spirits within them to come out. This is the beautiful concept behind the book *The Night Life of Trees.*

This is what Kodai has now captured with these lovely photos. The way these trees appear in the moonlight is wonderful — they may not look like this, during the day. And when you see these eerie shapes as you're walking along in the dark, you can easily imagine spirits living in them. Maybe that's why there are so many supernatural stories around trees.

K: I'm sure there must have been many stories at one point in time about every shinboku tree in our communities in Japan. But we no longer have anyone to tell these stories, like the Gond artists did in *The Night Life of Trees*.

B: The tree has become one of the main symbols in Gond art. This is powerful art, because it combines the rendering of a tree with stories, concepts and metaphors. Painting tree stories actually began with Jangarh Chacha. Give him any size of wall and he'd cover it with trees! He had a few stories that went with his paintings, not too many, but over time, more and more got added on.

We all began by observing him and helping him with his work, so trees became a big theme for us as well. We started to weave these stories into our narratives and then came *The Night Life of Trees*, which brought it all together.

K: I have thought of visible and invisible, day and night, sun and moon, light and shadow, as two sides to a coin, and in this sense, each completes each other. And so with a tree and its image.

Bhajju Shyam
Time
from Creation

Kodai (K): One of the stories that had struck
me when I read *The Night Life of Trees* was about
mahua. It's a kind of liquor made from the
fermented flowers of a tree by the same name —
and the Mahua tree itself is sacred, not just among
the Gonds, but in many adivasi communities.

Bhajju (B): In Gond tradition, the Mahua tree is like no other. Without mahua, no ceremonies can take place — it plays a role in births, deaths, weddings, festivals... almost all aspects of Gond life. In Ahir and Pardhan community religious rituals, we sprinkle mahua as a sacred offering to our gods. We do this during the last rites of the deceased as well, so that their soul can rest in peace.

Musicians anoint their instruments with mahua before they begin playing, and bhujrukhs — our bards and storytellers — invoke the blessings of the gods with mahua before they begin their singing. Mahua is considered sacred in Gond tradition.

Durga Bai
The Tree of Intoxication
from The Night Life of Trees

K: Until I visited Patan, I had only read about the Mahua tree. It's very special — the tree blooms for a period of two weeks, in March, around the time of the Holi festival. The flowers actually open at night, and drop their petals as the sun rises. If you listen carefully, you can hear the sound of the petals fall to the ground. How beautiful is that!

Women and children pick the petals up the next day, gathering them in big baskets. I picked one up and put it in my mouth. It tasted incredibly sweet.

Mahua liquor is made from these petals, and it's a slow, time-consuming process. Every house I visited offered me mahua to drink, almost always. Mahua isn't just any liquor, and the tree is not just a tree — they both have deep significance in Gond mythology and culture.

B: Mahua is a kind of wealth for the Gonds. The brew not only plays a sacred role in our culture, but it's also valuable in an economic sense. A lot of women sell mahua to make ends meet. If a farmer falls on hard times — sometimes through no fault of his own — Mahua trees are always something to fall back on, like insurance. People who have a Mahua tree in their yard are said to sit on wealth.

Unlike the uncertainty of a yearly harvest, a Mahua tree lives on for decades, and people rely on its generous by-products to earn a bit of money. We sell them, like we sell soya beans. But there is a big difference between our relationship to a Mahua tree, and to a newly introduced crop like soya. To be honest, we don't really know how to use soya in the village — we don't cook with it. I was given edamame once when I went abroad and discovered to my surprise that it was nothing but soya pods.

K: Rice has a similar significance in our culture. It used to be currency once, it was that important. Rice is still one of our staple foods, and Japanese *sake* is made from rice. We even have a ritual where rice is given as a sacred offering to our gods.

B: There's talk nowadays, that mahua is not such a good thing. It is equated with the alcohol that you can buy from a shop, and all the ill-effects that go with drinking. I'm not sure this comparison is a right one. Apart from its association with the sacred in Gond culture, there's also the fact that it is not made in large factories but by a slow, traditional home-made process, and mostly produced by women. Some of them don't even drink! They would check the quality of the mahua by sprinkling it on a fire, rather than taste it.

All in all, when you consider our deep and complex relationship to mahua, I hope that we can hold on to this valuable tradition.

Life · Animals

Kodai (K): Animals feature a lot in Gond painting, but the only ones I saw during my visit to Patan were birds and domestic animals like cows and goats, apart from a few small wild creatures.

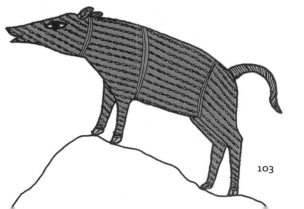

103

Bhajju (B): The jungle has moved steadily away from our village, because of development: trees have been cut, roads and houses built. I remember my father and others of his generation telling us that when they were young, the forest was a couple of kilometres from the village. They would tell us tales of bears, tigers and other wild animals they had encountered. These stories are part of our memories. In a way, we still live closely with animals, closer than people in the city — but these are domestic animals, as Kodai says.

Looking after animals is both "men's work" and "women's work". It used to be primarily a man's job to graze cattle, but now that so many men have migrated to the city, women have taken over these tasks easily. There is no choice. Even earlier, women would take over when men travelled.

There is an intimate relationship between the animals and the people who look after them. They feel comfortable with each other, there is a certain closeness, and people don't mind sharing their space with animals.

I still remember how we raised a tiny
calf that our cow had given birth to,
in our courtyard. Our animals eat and
sleep with us. Of course, this is only
possible in the more traditional houses.

K: The closeness that people have to animals in Patangarh is interesting. Artists from the village love to depict animals, both tame and wild. A good artist who paints animals — realistically or otherwise — is in some way familiar with that animal. How do animals move, walk, run, sleep, make love to each other? How are they when they are cautious, relaxed, or snuggling up to their mother? A familiarity and ease with animals brings out an essence that is true to their nature.

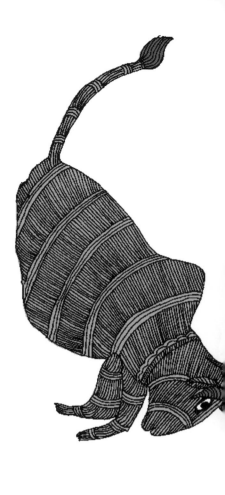

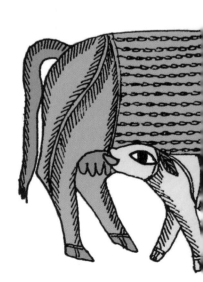

B: We know a lot about our animals, for instance, about how they experience time. Our knowledge comes from knowing life in the village, its rhythms and movements. Animals know when they will be fed, when they will be let out to graze... they also recognise and remember people, and can tell if you're from the village or outside it.

K: I once looked up at the sky in Patan, and saw birds flying overhead. I was surprised that they were flying exactly in the same way as Bhajju had depicted them, in one of his paintings.

The birds may not have been
painted realistically in Bhajju's paintings,
but his sense of them, taking flight
in the sky, was uncanny.

B: We are close to the animals that live with us in the village. But what about the wild ones which were once part of our lives and continue to be part of our imagination? As the forest recedes even further, any animals that are left must now be hidden deep inside. Our children in the cities only get to see wild animals shut up in cages in the zoo, where they're paraded as a spectacle, dependent entirely on humans. This is sad, that's not how they need to live.

Perhaps I belong to the last generation which has a recollection of animals in the wild. I remember, during my childhood, we would sometimes stay overnight in the fields with our families, during harvest time. We would hear foxes howling in the night. The howling was different from their usual sounds, and some elders would say that if a fox made that sound, it signified death.

Back then, animals were part of our world and life, not only as creatures in themselves, but with meaning and significance which then became part of our myths and stories. Snakes came to signify the earth, fish stood in for water...

We've never forgotten these tales of jungle animals, which have been handed to us over generations.

They are very much alive in our memories, and have become part of Gond consciousness. It is not accidental that Gond art is filled with animals.

Some animals are depicted more than others and that's because artists love painting them, and they are popular with people who buy Gond art.

Life · Celebration

Bhajju (B): We Gonds just need an excuse to celebrate, we love festivities! We're always ready to eat, drink, sing and dance.

B: We work hard all year round, and hardly have time to be with each other in the old way. But when festivals come around, we really like letting loose and catching up with everyone — and what better place than Patangarh? Most people living in the city try to return to the village for the major festivals, even if they can't make it to every single one that comes up during the year. Festivals in the village are legendary, from the thorough preparations to the wholehearted way everyone joins in on the special day. Festivals are where our community life thrives.

The two major festivals in Patangarh are Holi and Diwali, which mark the beginning of spring and the coming of winter. They were originally Hindu festivals, but we have our own adivasi versions, which are a mix of different rituals. Each festival has its own set of songs in our language, and practices particular to us. Some traditions are different from that of the cities, but some are the same.

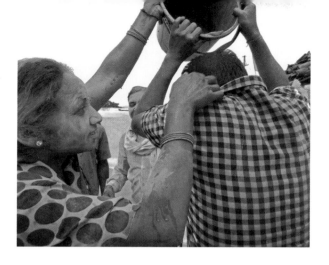

Holi is a festival of colours at Patangarh, just like everywhere else. People throw colours at each other, and there is great merriment.

I always try to celebrate Holi in the village, whenever possible, and it was during Holi that Kodai visited me.

Kodai (K): I was so happy to come to Patangarh with Bhajju for Holi. It took me back to the days when I was a child. I would excitedly wait for festival days, any festival. It was so exciting, we hung out with friends, visited food stalls around temples, and listened to 'matsuri-bayashi' — traditional Japanese festival music.

राजूनरा जूलाई
१४ माई ते ८वर्ष केबच्चो को प्रत्येह ६ माह
विटामिन A का धोल ६ अवश्य पिलाये

B: When I come to Patan to celebrate Holi, I am usually given a drum — called 'timki' — to play. It's a mark of respect to ask an arriving guest to drum, a kind of honour. I have to say though, that we try to avoid giving it to guests who are really clueless about drumming. We might ask half-heartedly out of custom and politeness, but hope that the guest — if he doesn't know how to play — will decline!

Speaking for myself, I'm not a musician, but growing up in the village and watching my father play, I have come to be steeped in the tradition. So I am not a bad drummer.

My grandfather used to play a stringed instrument and sometimes called me to accompany him. I used to pluck vaguely at the strings because I didn't know how to play it, but he believed that I'd slowly learn by immersing myself in the experience.

But I have to say that it feels a bit strange to be regarded as a "guest" in the village and be given a drum... but my spirits lift as soon as my sister, who lives in Patan, starts to sing and dance.

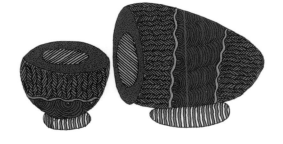

117

B: We've grown up with songs since we were tiny. They are really ancient, and the same basic song can vary in lyrics, tunes and meaning from village to village. In fact, in our village, each family has their own version of any particular song. When we were growing up, we would sit alongside our parents when they sang during festival time, and they'd encourage us to join in — almost like a refrain. So you're really schooled into this performance, and get good at it. Each family in the community has their own particular nuances: a son would pick up his father's special rendering.

There is also a lot of community singing. As for dance, everyone dances, young and old. It's hard to describe the infectious spirit in words, so I'm glad Kodai has captured these moments.

Every time I go to the village for Holi, every child in the village forces me to dance and sing all the time. I'd sit down to catch my breath, only to be accosted by a gang of children begging and demanding that I get up and dance. The only difference to when I was a child is the fact that recorded traditional songs now blast out of huge speakers that people have set up.

These joyous singing and dancing sessions during Holi are one aspect of Gond culture. There are also other — more formal and ceremonial — dances that are part of village festivals.

I've actually been greatly inspired by dance traditions of the village in my own art. My "detailing" — the pattern that I use to fill the figures in my paintings — is inspired by a dance called 'Saila'. It's an interlinked chain, standing in for the men and women linking hands during a Saila dance. It's an important symbol of Gond tradition for me, and links me to community life in Patangarh.

B: Another particular tradition in Patangarh, which children really look forward to, is a big bonfire in the night called 'Holikaa'. Older people set things up for them in the evening, and then the children take over.

Wood is now hard to come by, so bits of hay and wood splinters are used. Neighbouring villages compete with each other to see whose bonfire is the best.

K: Even in Japan, a festival night was one where children were allowed to step into the world in the dark, by themselves. So I understood the excitement that kids in Patangarh felt on the night of Holikaa.

When the bonfire roared up about three meters high, the children shouted 'Holikaa!' keeping time with the beating drums. Behind the bonfire, I saw a big Peepal tree illuminated by a full moon.

B: As night approaches, you can actually see which village in the area has already lit their bonfire, and how large it is.

As a child, I remember collecting the ashes from the fire the next day since it was considered sacred. These ashes were actually one of the important "original" colours that you play with during Holi.

Children stay up all night, watching the bonfire burn and on the morning after Holikaa, it's a familiar sight to see them all huddled together, asleep. I have to mention that there's a pesky custom of poking sleeping people with a burning twig, which probably explains why some children choose to hide behind a mound.

K: Colour was slowly coming back into the world by the time the Holikaa flames went out. Just before the sun came up on the horizon, I saw a beautiful pink tinted sky.

Thinking back to the Holi festival, the image of Bhajju — drenched in colours, singing and pounding the drum — suddenly made me connect different things. Painting, drumming, singing: they are all in his blood, born as he is into the community of performing arts, the Pardhan Gonds. All this makes him the artist that he is.

Abstract Art from Lived Life

Tara Books: The sheer number of artists who have emerged from Patangarh and its neighbouring villages is astonishing. Their work is rich and symbolic, revolving around the myths, legends and beliefs of the community. Their style of rendering is intricate and detailed, inspired by the decorative and practical arts of the village. Unique to the art form are the decorative patterns that fill the paintings. These intricate marks are not there to simply enhance the graphic quality of the painting, like shading or cross-hatching. Each pattern actually has a special meaning — inspired by some aspect of life in the village — and has been individually created by the artist. Each artist has a small repertoire of personal patterns that he or she uses — and to someone familiar with the different artists, it is possible to identify who he or she is, by looking at the detailing in the painting. The pattern is their signature, so to speak.

Some years ago, interested in discovering more about this unique practice, we published a book called *Signature*. We collected a large number of paintings from a range of artists, and looked closely at the patterns which filled them. We then asked each artist to comment on why they had come up with a particular design and what they said was revelatory. They had been inspired by nature, work, festivities and daily life... but also by communal memory, time, tradition and imagination.

I've followed the lines, the lines from the
past to the present, tracing memory.

Narmada Prasad Tekam

A thatched roof is what I have in mind.

Prasad Kusaram

I've used a garland of leaves. I've been inspired by the
floor paintings done by the women in our village.

Ramsingh Urveti

Have you seen a muzzle on a bull?
That's what I've used as a design.

Kala Santosh Vyam

A rope woven together, when you look closely, makes my design.

Rajendra Shyam

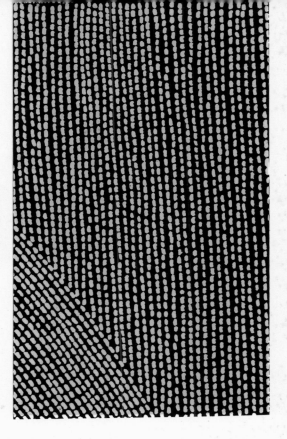

When you plough a field, you leave marks on the earth, and that makes my pattern.

Nikki Singh Urveti

This is from the jewellery that we wear, from an amulet with a pattern of paddy seeds.

Durga Bai

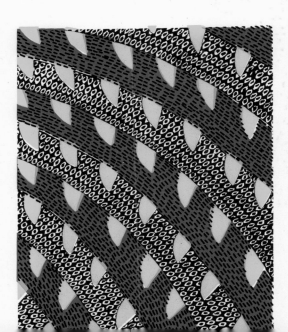

This is the design
of a tattoo.

Jyothi Bai

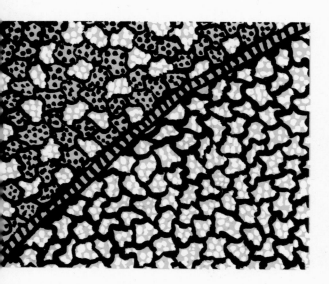

This is the pattern that a cow makes
on the earth with her hooves.

Pradeep Marawe

These are seeds, scattered
on the feathers of a peacock.

Subhash Vyam

This is the pattern created by a marriage procession,
as it weaves through the village.

Nankusiya Shyam

My pattern is made up of a group
of dancers, seen from above.

Bhajju Shyam

We were amazed at what they had achieved through their patterns — which was nothing less than a carefully considered turning of lived experience into abstract designs, by a community of artists. To us, at the time, this stood in for the conceptual genius of this art form.

That still holds true. But what this book has allowed us to do is to take our exploration further — to revisit the practice of detailing which we originally published in *Signature* — and extend our understanding of its meanings. As we held images of life in the village in front of us, the connections between life worlds and art practice acquired an unprecedented authenticity and immediacy. We discovered that many of the themes of this book unerringly matched the inspirations for the patterns that Pardhan Gond artists have created. Seen in this light, these patterns embody the connection between lived life and abstract art with extraordinary sophistication.

Kodai (K): In my opinion, the nature of art is that it gives some sort of order to chaos. For the Gond people, I think, drawing trees does that. They "discovered" their stories within trees which in turn were rooted in their daily lives.

Bhajju (B): Most people in Patangarh are farmers. If I think about our early relationship to "art" in the old days, say, before Jangarh Chacha started painting in Bhopal, and many of us became artists painting on canvas, I would say we were always interested in making things, most of which were useful.

Our relationship to material was very organic and local — we worked with wood, clay, fibre and to some extent, metal. People would make agricultural tools, rope, furniture, fish traps or build houses.

Growing up in the village, you realised that making things involved not only your hands, but your whole body.

It was a physical act, and you got a sense of materials, how they behaved, and how to use your tools in the best possible way. Some of these tools looked very simple, but you could use them to work with fibre, wood, bamboo... and you could make everything with them, from rope to fishnets!

B: And now when I look back, I can see how every single person in the village had some kind of art — 'kala' — in his or her hands.

This may not be "art" or "craft" in the way that the marketplace recognises it, but I see it more as a way of being creative with material: completely involved in what you're making, and doing it extremely well. I'm now a fairly well-known artist, but I can't plaster a wall with mud in the beautifully refined way some women in the village can.

گو

B: There is expertise in what they made, and how they went about it. My father, for example, made the best ploughs in the village. He was renowned for it, and everyone in the community wanted one made by him. His ploughs were strong and well-crafted — he would design each one specially, depending on the size of the bull.

There's another important thing I want to mention about the objects made in the village: apart from their usefulness, many of the things people made were also beautiful. This addition of what you could perhaps call "unnecessary" decoration — because the thing can be used even when it's plain — is due to a basic creative impulse. This is why I say that these people were all artists, in their own way. They had an appreciation of beauty, even in making and using mundane everyday things.

K: Images and the stories the Gond people tell reveal the invisible, and this gives us a new perspective on the world. This is true of legends and folklore across cultures. Rather effortlessly, they carry traces of the invisible. Sadly, this is not something that appears possible in a highly modernised world. But I think, to the Gond people, the border between visible and invisible is still rather seamless. And this is also why perhaps life is not too different from art, and maybe it is a kind of living art.

B: The impulse to beautify everyday things is behind some of the decorative work in the courtyards and the relief murals on house walls. The practice was to create motifs on the bottom and top halves of walls, leaving the middle free. Working on these motifs was my first introduction as a youngster to art making: I would help my mother paint the top bits that she found hard to reach.

It was always the women of the household who would make the murals, and decorate the courtyards. I was really happy they let me help, because I enjoyed doing this work a lot — I'm not sure I even thought of it as work, it was so pleasurable.

This brings me to something else I want to say about creativity in Patangarh — sometimes people would make things with no real "use", just for pleasure, for fun. When you sat around in the evening, you could see people returning home with the cattle they had taken out to graze and with their food baskets on their heads. And in these baskets you'd find wood carvings at which they had perhaps whittled away all day. Back in the day, there was no idea of selling these wooden figures — it was just something you did, to pass the time and for sheer fun.

Things have changed quite a bit since those days, and the arts in Patan have taken off in a different direction. But I would say there are still a few people left who continue to nurture their creative sides in an everyday sense, as they go about farming or grazing. As for me, it's the things I've described here which have gone into making me the artist I am today.

Art · Floor

Bhajju (B): My own interest in painting started when I began helping my mother decorate those parts of our walls that she couldn't reach easily. Ever since then — even though my own career as an artist has taken me in very different directions — I have always been fascinated by the floor and wall art that women in the village create. Floor art is called 'digna'. It's my belief that digna is the alphabet of Gond art — it is from this ancient practice that our art has grown.

B: There's a Gond story of creation: in the beginning, there was just water. Then the great god Bada Dev dreamt of land, with trees, animals and humans living on it. So he took some mud, and started spreading it on the water with his hands and that's how the earth was born. It seems to me that the act of creating a digna mimics and honours that first creation.

A digna is considered auspicious, and plays a large role in the cultural life of our community. There are countless types of digna, and each one has its own name and purpose. There are special ones created for every significant occasion, from birth to marriage to death. There are intricate dignas for special festivals, but also simple ones for everyday. Dignas are constantly re-made, because they are by nature temporary.

Bhajju Shyam
Digna
from Between Memory and Museum:
A Dialogue with Folk and Tribal Artists

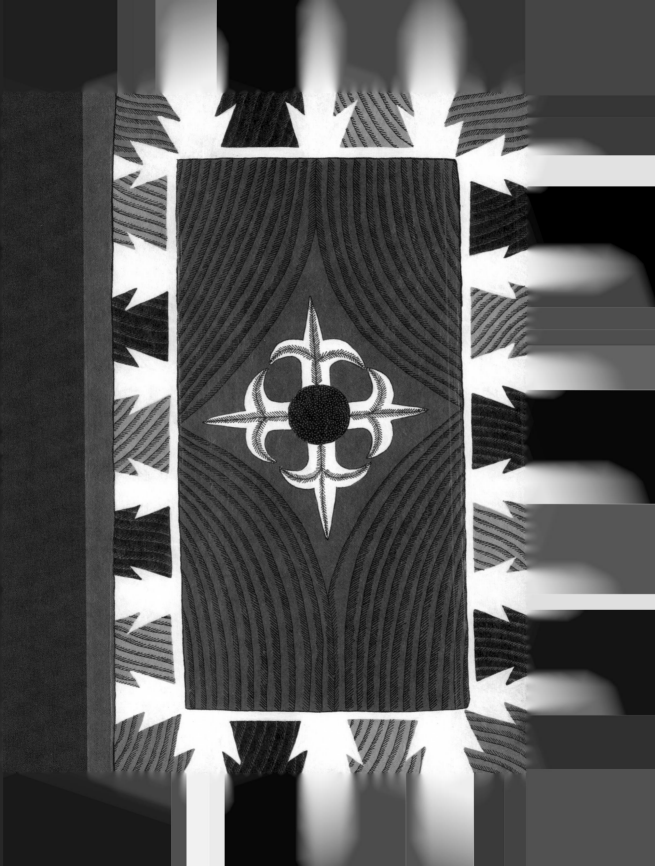

Kodai (K): I was told that digna designs were handed down from mother to daughter. Yet you don't ever find the same digna — each artist appears to have her unique signature and style. The art of the digna is not static, and grows endlessly.

Bhajju Shyam
Unpublished illustration
for Creation

B: It is believed that good fortune will only enter your home when there is a beautiful digna on the threshold. It's a matter of pride for women, and a reflection on their housekeeping skills. Noticing and commenting on each other's dignas is common village practice. Some women are of course considered much better at it than others.

B: You begin a digna with clearing and preparing the ground — mostly the courtyard of homes — with a layer of fresh cow dung. So a proper digna can only be made in a village home (or community square) which has the space and materials the women need for their work. I realised this connection between the art form and its location when I moved to Bhopal. There is no space for digna in Bhopal. The only ones we get to see in the city are models in museums and craft villages.

Once the ground is prepared, women start working on creating decorative designs using a paste of lime and chalk. It is squeezed through the fingers, sometimes with a piece of cloth. Traditionally, these white designs would also be filled in with different earth colours — white, black, yellow, red or green mud. Nowadays, of course, it's hard to source this kind of natural coloured earth, so some women have taken to mixing commercial colours into their white paste, especially when they decorate walls.

I'm always amused that women don't seem to mind ruining their hands when they're decorating their homes for festivals... even if they're wearing brand new clothes on the special occasion! They're quite comfortable with themselves, and quite unselfconscious. Beautifying the home is hard work, but perhaps, for them that is more important than anything else.

B: The tough manual labour that is part of village life is evident in making a digna as well. It's a very physical activity: the whole body is used, and you need a good sense of balance while you're twisting your body to move carefully through the (still wet) design, even as you create it. You move inside the work. A woman has to literally take control of the space.

I'm always amazed at how they mentally measure the space, and scale the work accordingly. They don't sketch it out first — they just put in the border, and then it's all free hand, evolving as they go along.
On one hand, the scale is so large, and on the other hand, the fingers move with great delicacy. When you watch a digna taking shape, slowly, you notice how absorbed the women are, and how they're enjoying it.

B: While a digna is quite temporary, wall art has a longer life. It also begins with cleaning and preparing the walls.

The tradition probably started with extending the digna to the walls, but then took on a life of its own, like applying straight blocks of colour along the entire length of a wall.

The practice of making a relief — like a three-dimensional mural — with animal or human figures is quite ancient, though.

You can see some of these traditional figures in a few of the old houses that are still standing. Jangarh Chacha's grandmother's home has a fine example of a piece that she made.

People still create wall art, much of it inspired by the old designs, but also much that is new. What I really like about the wall art is the fact that people seem to make it simply for their own pleasure, like in a cowshed, or the back of a house where no one is likely to see it!

Even though contemporary Gond art has taken off in a completely new direction, I still see — and greatly value — its origins in the everyday traditional art of women in the village. If you see Jangarh Chacha's early works, they are simple, and clearly inspired by the digna. That, combined with the wall art, was what started him off. Over a period of time, he began to bring in our stories and myths into his complex paintings.

As for me, I keep coming back to the digna — not just as a form which gave rise to current Gond painting — but as a deep and sophisticated form in its own right. I've tried to understand more about its philosophy, and also to see where it can be taken, as itself. I've organised several workshops with women, where we've tried to paint digna on canvas, to see where it goes… I'm not sure how successful this is, or where it will take us, but I remain fascinated.

K: It was such a privilege to be able to watch women creating this beautiful art on the ground. The designs were amazing, and the women clearly enjoyed this painting ritual. This was particularly moving because they knew how temporary their work would be: people would step on it, and it would fade with wind and weather. It was really an art of the moment. Still they made them, over and over.

I couldn't help but think of birth and death, as if the digna was telling me to live in and enjoy this moment, in fact, every moment, fully.

This is also why I am so helplessly drawn to this country! It gives me the power to believe in life, in continuity and in creativity.

Art · Wood

Bhajju (B): Digna is one way of beautifying our homes. Traditionally, the other way has been through decorative wood work. This was particularly so in some houses in Patan, in what I would like to call artists' houses.

B: Sadly, though, much of this work belongs to the past, when craftsmen were highly respected and people used to depend on their expertise to build houses. They were not what people in the city call "carpenters". They were actually *mistris*, masons whose skill lay in building traditional homes. For instance, there is a wooden pillar we call a 'chirai' which holds up the structure of the entire house. It's shaped like the wings of a sparrow. A traditional craftsman would not only calculate the strength and technical details of the pillar, but also fashion it beautifully, with intricate details.

He would decide on the design of the doors, and how they ought to be carved, so he had a say not only in how the house was built, but how it looked, aesthetically.

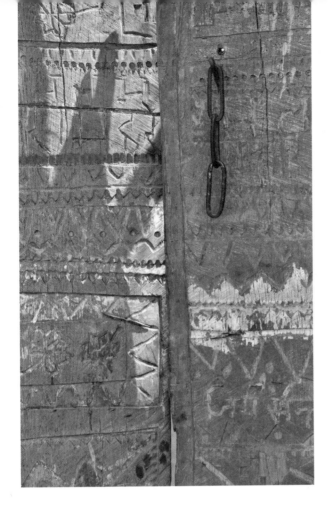

B: There is not much work for wood craftsmen now, because everyone is building concrete structures. The new houses don't have wooden pillars any more, they've been replaced by concrete ones. Craftsmen who were once renowned for building mud houses are now hired as labourers.

They cannot be expected to build entire houses in some other material.

The problem is that wood itself is hard to source now. There's a tree called Bamool which is grown in the village now, for cheap wood. They say that nothing grows under

170

the shade of the Bamool tree, and that's true. But because there's no other wood in the village, people tend to grow and sell Bamool wood.

So what kind of work do craftsmen take on these days? It really depends. Perhaps making some window frames for the new houses, or maybe some basic furniture. Or wedding canopies.

B: The traditional skill of wood craftsmen continues to be useful and valuable, when it comes to making wooden masks and idols. Once a year, there's a festival called 'Chherta', during which people — mostly children — put these masks on and play. They go from door to door calling out "chherta! chherta!" and ask for grains and produce from each house. Then everyone goes to the pond and cooks and eats a big meal. One of the items that must be eaten that day is a crow and one person is assigned this task.

Craftsmen make idols of our gods and goddesses from their imagination, because we don't have any images of our gods to fall back on. So all of them are born from the craftsmen's creativity.

Kodai (K): I visited a wood carver called Chatura Urveti during my visit to Patangarh, and he showed me a mask he had carved. He said: 'One night I dreamt of Mahalarin and this is what he looked like in my dream.' Mahalarin, a local god, is said to live on the outskirts of the village. The villagers' faith in Mahalarin is strong, but there are no idols or images of him. When we think of different gods — Vishnu, Shiva or the Buddha — we have immediate visual associations. But the mask looked like nothing I'd ever seen before. It did look like an 'Oni' — a Japanese ogre — but I'm sure that was just a coincidence!

K: Chatura Urveti said that his Mahalarin looked the way it did because of that one dream and added: 'If I have another dream of Mahalarin, it may look different.'
In Patangarh I saw the origin of spirituality in formlessness — a faith without figures.

B: Chatura Urveti is a master craftsman and he's done a lot of good work. He's around my age, and travels all around the country showing and selling his wooden masks and figures. Sometimes he's invited by the government to hold workshops and training programs for wood craftsmen. But the strange thing is that even though he's a fantastic craftsman, he's building a new concrete house — he doesn't have the wood to repair his old house!

Like I said before, there used to be a time when farmers who were artistically inclined would make rough wood carvings just for the pleasure of doing so. They were not necessarily professional wood craftsmen. Some of the figures they came up with were from their own imagination, and just playfully done. So, for example, a man might do a carving of, say, a woman from a neighbouring tribe, maybe a Baiga woman. This does not mean he had actually seen the woman. And, if shown this carving, the woman might not even recognise herself! But there he was, carving away, and in a particular style.

B: Over a period of time, I think people working with wood — artistic people, as well as professional wood craftsmen — started observing each other's work and started to form a distinctive style of wooden sculpture. Some of it is more tribal in style and subject matter, and some more general and "commercial". They began to sell these pieces whenever they travelled, inspired by the way Gond painters sell their canvases.

Unlike paintings, selling wooden sculptures has proved to be really hard. They are heavy and cumbersome to transport, and buyers are few. Aware of how commercially successful Gond painting has become, most wood craftsmen have switched to painting. It's an interesting relationship: they have brought many of the wood carving and hatching techniques into their painting — while some of them have taken the patterns and detailing of Gond painting onto wood!

Bhajju (B): It was Jangarh Chacha who started the tradition of painting we all practise now. He took the decorative arts of the village like digna and wall murals in a new direction. His work was influenced by these traditional styles, but the subject matter was completely new: he began to paint the stories, myths and beliefs of the Gonds. When I first worked with him — filling in the details in his paintings — I couldn't really understand what he was doing. It was so different from village art!

B: He told me how important it was to keep the old stories alive, as a Pardhan Gond. We belong to a sub-sect of the Gonds called Pardhan: at one time, Pardhans used to be the priests and singers of the community. They would go from village to village, and people would invite them to perform important rituals, recite genealogies and the ancient creation myths. Over time, this changed due to various reasons, and the Pardhans lost their calling, turning into poor farmers, just like the others.

But there are still some individuals — the bhujrukhs — who still keep these performances alive in the old way. A bhujrukh is a keeper of traditional stories and beliefs — but seen in a broader sense, he's also an old man who's seen the world, and has some wisdom to impart.

Kodai (K): When I was a child, I remember storytellers called 'biwa-hoshi' in Japan. They were blind priests who played the 'biwa' — a Japanese lute — as they moved around the towns and countryside, narrating stories to people. They were a bit like bhujrukhs, which is probably why I felt there was something familiar about them!

B: It's hard to even find a bhujrukh now — the last time I had to scout around the area for a couple of days before finding someone to perform at my house. There are just two bhujrukhs left in Patangarh, and they're quite old. They're rarely invited by individual families anymore. A community might call them, or they give performances in museums or government institutions. Fortunately, one of them was ready to take up my invitation.

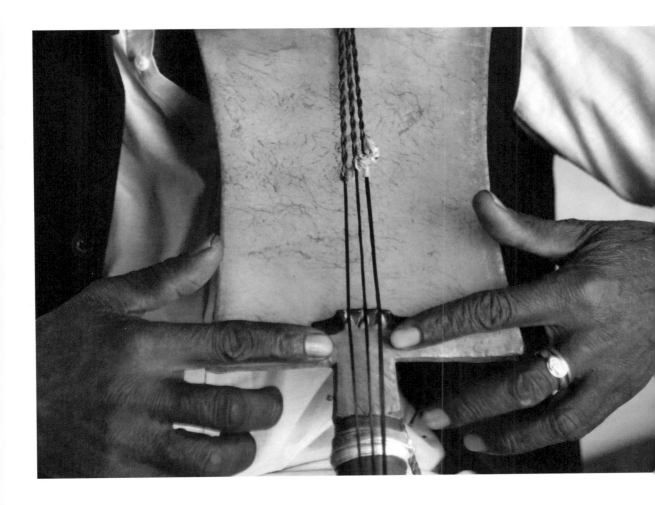

K: Bhajju told me that this bhujrukh, Balaram Ayam, was one of the few genuine ones left in Patangarh. The bhujrukh accompanies himself with a stringed instrument called 'bana', which he makes himself. The strings are made with horse hair, usually a very specific number like 40 or 60, and there's a story as to why this is so. The performance that I witnessed lasted all night, accompanied by glasses of mahua.

Appropriately enough, Ayam narrated the story of a Gond king and queen who ruined themselves by drinking and were forced into exile!

It turned out that even Bhajju hadn't heard this story before. He wondered what they did when they got out of exile… did they live in the forest forever? Is that where the Baigas — whom Gonds consider their "cousins" — come from?

B: A bhujrukh needs a good audience and an inviting space to perform well. The people who gather around him are part of the performance, asking questions and ready with repartees.

I was very lucky to grow up with bhujrukh performances throughout my childhood. And I know that Jangarh Chacha was fond of travelling around with a bhujrukh, and learnt a lot from him. But these traditions were much stronger then.

I fear that after these few men pass on, that will be the end of this tradition. The knowledge they hold is invaluable and because it is oral, and not written down, we may seriously lose it. It is particularly crucial for us artists, because Gond art now is based on the old stories and beliefs.

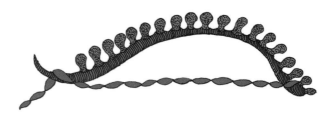

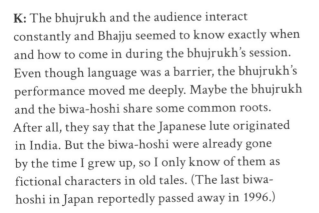

K: The bhujrukh and the audience interact constantly and Bhajju seemed to know exactly when and how to come in during the bhujrukh's session. Even though language was a barrier, the bhujrukh's performance moved me deeply. Maybe the bhujrukh and the biwa-hoshi share some common roots. After all, they say that the Japanese lute originated in India. But the biwa-hoshi were already gone by the time I grew up, so I only know of them as fictional characters in old tales. (The last biwa-hoshi in Japan reportedly passed away in 1996.)

B: There are some artists from Patangarh — women like Chandrakali Pusam or Durga Bai, for example — who have grown up with bhujrukhs in their families. They are great storytellers themselves and understand the meaning and symbolism behind what they paint. They know which ceremonial song to sing on what occasion. And when they sell a painting, they're able to narrate the entire story it depicts. Not every artist can. Sometimes, when someone asks us for the deeper meaning behind a painting, we don't know what to say beyond a point.

Even I don't know all there is to know — maybe artists still living in Patangarh know and remember more than those who have moved to the city.

I have to say though, that extensive knowledge of the old stories doesn't necessarily translate into better paintings — Durga Bai is, of course, an exception.

Durga Bai
The Museum as Mother
from Between Memory and Museum:
A Dialogue with Folk and Tribal Artists

But many times, it's entirely possible
for someone to be a master storyteller
without being a master painter. Knowing
what parts of a story translate well into a
painting is important for a good artist.

What is clear is that for our arts and culture
to be rooted, and to continue to grow, we
need to nurture the keepers of this tradition.

The bhujrukh and his knowledge has been
the source of our art as it exists now.
I'm not sure how many people even within
the Gond community realise that, so that's
where the education needs to begin.

As of now, apart from a few bhujrukhs,
it does look as though our legacy is in peril.
A couple of museums have a few recordings,
and I have some personal recordings
too. That's all we'll be left with if things
continue this way. Added to which
recordings can never recreate the live
interactive nature of a bhujrukh session.
No performance is like any other.

Ramsingh Urveti
The Tree of Song
from The Night Life of Trees

K: In Patangarh, the bhujrukh still sings the story of their people, as did his father and his grandfather before him. But the danger is that he will be forgotten in no time, and just become a vague memory of the past. It looks like the bhujrukh I met was the last of his kind in Patan.

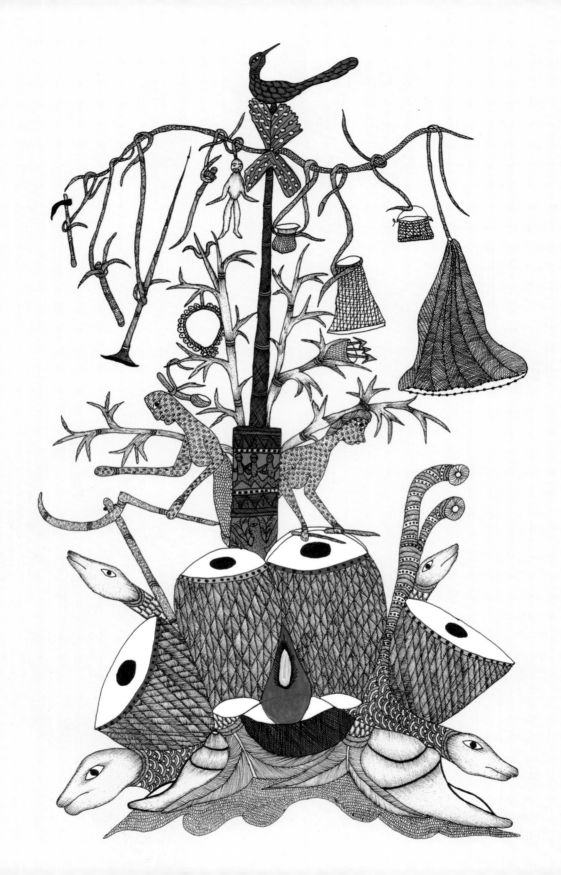

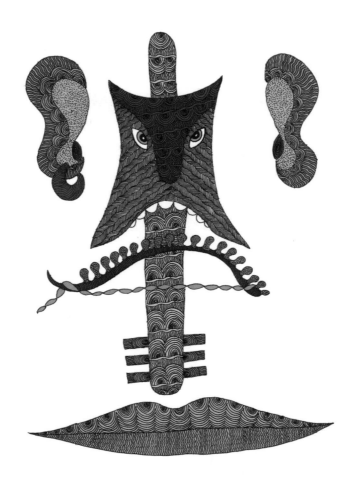

B: So how do we preserve this tradition? I'm very keen on it. I make sure to invite a bhujrukh regularly to my place, and call the entire neighbourhood. I try to listen carefully, ask questions and make recordings. But I'm not sure that's enough. So I've been working on this idea of a workshop or get-together for bhujrukhs in our area, followed by recordings and competitions? Such an initiative might raise some curiosity or interest in some of the younger men to learn the art. Perhaps we could arrange some kind of stipend for them to learn it part-time, perhaps in the evening after work.

But these ideas need support, and from governmental and non-governmental organisations. If such support is forthcoming, then our younger generation could be enlisted in learning the art of the bhujrukh.

Such efforts are necessary and vital for the future of Gond culture and art. We need a strong link to the past, even as we set off in new directions as artists.

Prasad Singh Kusharam
Badadev
from Between Memory and Museum:
A Dialogue with Folk and Tribal Artists

Dhavat Singh Uikey
Tiger Memories
from Where has the Tiger Gone?

The Legacy of Jangarh Singh Shyam

Bhajju: Patangarh's most famous son is the great artist Jangarh Singh Shyam. He was my uncle. Unfortunately, he died young — we were shocked when he took his own life under tragic circumstances during a residency in Japan. I don't think we have got over it even today. But what can we do, except try to keep his memory alive, in our hearts, but also in Patangarh, where his ancestral house still stands? He was living in this house when the group sent by Swaminathan — the contemporary artist and museum director from Bharat Bhavan in Bhopal — came to Patangarh in their search for talented local artists. They saw a green mural that Jangarh Chacha had painted on his wall, and decided that it showed a lot of promise. So they invited him to come to Bharat Bhavan right away, where they gave him a studio space and materials.

In Bhopal, he began to paint on paper and canvas, and did something very new with this material: he began to turn the Gond stories and myths he had heard from the bhujrukh and other Pardhan Gond elders in the village into paintings. Such a thing had never been done before. Jangarh Chacha was also inspired by digna and the other arts from the village, but in his paintings, they became something else. You could say that this was the beginning of what people know today as "Gond painting". Many young artists were inspired by his work, and he didn't mind this at all. He was the most generous man I have ever known. He encouraged youngsters from the village to come to Bhopal, and taught them everything he knew. I was one of these young people, and began my career as an artist by filling in the details in his paintings.

After he moved to Bhopal, Jangarh Chacha would occasionally bring foreign visitors to the village, and they'd stay with him in his ancestral house.

I was really young then and I remember taking visitors
to the river to bathe, since there was no water in the
village at the time. Even though no one has lived in
Jangarh Chacha's old house in Patan for a while, we still keep
it up — repairing and redecorating it during festival times.
His immediate family, including his brothers, used to live
together there when he was alive. But after he passed away,
his brothers moved out, and now Jangarh Chacha's wife,
son and daughter have moved to Bhopal as well. They have
become practising artists. Visitors to Patan do come to see his
old house, and there is talk of converting it into a museum.
I really hope that happens. You could say that Gond art —
and artists — wouldn't exist in this form if it wasn't for him.

Jangarh Chacha helped everyone out. There were five
other young men working as his apprentices before
I joined him. I had actually gone to Bhopal to find work
on my own — not with the intention of painting or
becoming an artist — so I didn't join him right away.
I had all kinds of jobs initially — I was a security guard,
a night watchman, an electrician's helper, a gardener,
a casual labourer... then one day, Jangarh Chacha came
to my place, and asked me to come around and help him
at his studio. I didn't have a permanent job and I was
single, so all I really cared about was having a place
to stay and some food to eat — so I agreed.

Jangarh Chacha taught me everything I needed to know.
I started out by filling colour into his paintings, and I had
to be very careful to stay within his intricate black and
white lines. His work was getting well-known, and orders
were coming in all the time. So he would rapidly come up
with images in black and white, and ask his apprentices
to fill in the colours. Sometimes, we'd work through the
night to finish paintings to meet urgent deadlines.

We learnt through watching him at work. It's not that he
knew everything: there were many things that he himself
was experimenting with, like mixing colours, for instance.
He'd have a specific colour in mind but didn't know how
to go about making it — none of us knew, really.

Jangarh Singh Shyam
Tigers
from Beasts of India

Colours were very expensive at the time, so we had to be careful. Sometimes Jangarh Chacha would keep adding colour upon colour to correct a particular mix, and by the end of it all, he'd come up with litres of paint in a colour he didn't even want. And then he'd tell us: take this colour and go paint that wall!

The thing is, whatever Jangarh Chacha told us, he never felt that he was the authority on the subject of Gond art. We never talked about our tradition in a formal way. He actually learnt along the way, as he created his own form of art — in fact we all did, working along with him. It evolved through doing. We were of course aware of the different aspects of our culture: digna, murals, songs, storytelling, festivals… and we would join in during those occasions when Jangarh Chacha sang like a bhujrukh. He had a passion for the harmonium and the flute. But the important point is that he brought all these cultural forms together, into a way of painting that was his own creation, from his own imagination. Our gods don't have a form, so he'd paint them out of his imagination. When someone came to buy a painting, he would always tell them that the image was his own conception of the gods.

The main thing — the important thing — is that he didn't want us to stay his apprentices forever. He encouraged us to start painting on our own. Of course we were all influenced by the new form of painting he had created, and he was not against that. But even if we followed in his footsteps, he encouraged us to find a style that was unique to each of us. Otherwise you'll just become another me, he used to say. I really appreciate and understand the gravity of that now.

But at that time, I didn't reflect too much — I just started painting. And I discovered that I enjoyed it so much that it was hard to stop. So much so that my friends began teasing me for working all the time: was I suddenly taking myself too seriously as a painter? But then I ended up selling those paintings, and it felt very good to have the extra money to spend. So I kept at it, and after about two years into this, Jangarh Chacha pulled me aside and said I should seriously think of doing my own work, I should set out on my own. And that's what I did. And it was entirely due to him that I found my own style… today, I'm recognised for it.

Kodai: I once had the chance to look at a family tree of the Shyams, following their relationship to Jangarh Singh Shyam. I discovered that most Gond artists are related, in some way. Bhajju calls Jangarh "Chacha" or Uncle, with respect and affection, even though Jangarh was not his direct maternal or paternal uncle. This tight, close bonding in Indian families is not something we see in Japan. Jangarh took care of young Bhajju, inviting him to assist with his painting work, and mentoring him sensitively. We know how Bhajju benefited from that apprenticeship, and how he went on to become a great artist in his own right.

The art that Jangarh came up with has passed down directly to Bhajju and his generation of artists. Growing up in the village close to nature, listening to the bhujrukh sing, taking part in the crafts and festivities of the village, watching women folk decorate homes… all this fed into Jangarh's work. And he was generous in passing on what he knew.

It is then maybe not a coincidence that to me, Jangarh and Bhajju's paintings instantly communicate a dynamic and uplifting spirit — joy and meaning radiate from their images. I feel it is because they are both visual griots of traditional Gond folklore — and the fact that they have been part of that culture during their formative years in Patangarh has been a true blessing for them. They belong to a special generation, with one foot in the old traditions of the village and one in the modernity of the city.

What will it be like for the next generation of Gond artists? How will the art move forward for these young people who were born and brought up in the city, but still have pride in their ancestral traditions? Perhaps new forms of art will be born.

Illustrations

The illustrations featured in this book are
from various Tara Books titles, published over the years.

Front and back covers, endsheets, pages 3, 7 (TOP), 17 (TOP LEFT),
45, 48, 49, 68, 80, 108, 109, 111 (LEFT) and 197
Illustrations by Bhajju Shyam from **Creation (2014)**

Pages 7, 73 and 97
Illustrations by Ramsingh Urveti, Durga Bai and Ramsingh Urveti
from **The Night Life of Trees (2006)**

Pages 17 (TOP RIGHT), 18, 33, 89, 99, 110 (RIGHT), 116, 140, 180 and 198
Illustrations by Bhajju Shyam from **The London Jungle Book (2004)**

Contents page, pages 14, 25, 31, 32, 34, 35, 40, 41,
60, 61, 66, 105, 139, 149, 159, 161 and 175
Illustrations by Subhash Vyam from **Water (2017)**

Pages 17 (BOTTOM), 36, 103 (BOTTOM), 114–115, 127, 137, 179, 194, 199 (BOTTOM) and imprint page
Illustrations by Bhajju Shyam from **That's How I See Things (2007)**

Pages 20, 103 (TOP), 106–107 (CENTRE PIECE, BOTTOM), 147 and 193
Illustrations by Bhajju Shyam from **Alone in the Forest (2012)**

Pages 39, 46, 51, 55, 57, 71, 101, 102 (TOP AND BOTTOM), 107 (RIGHT), 113, 122, 157, 162 and 170
Illustrations by Durga Bai from **The Churki-Burki Book of Rhyme (2010)**

Pages 53 (RIGHT), 69, 78, 79, 119, 121, 143, 145, 165, 167 and 189
Illustrations by Bhajju Shyam, Dilip Shyam, Pradeep Marawe, Bhajju Shyam, Bhajju Shyam,
Ramsingh Urveti, Bhajju Shyam, Ramsingh Urveti, Bhajju Shyam and Dilip Shyam
from **Between Memory and Museum: A Dialogue with Folk and Tribal Artists (2015)**

Pages 53 (LEFT), 76, 110 (LEFT), 117, 125, 183 and 184
Illustrations by Dhavat Singh Uikey from **Where has the Tiger Gone? (2018)**

Pages 102 (CENTRE), 106 (LEFT), 106–107 (CENTRE PIECE, TOP) and 111 (RIGHT)
Illustrations by Nankusiya Shyam, Ramsingh Urveti, Durga Bai and Bhajju Shyam
from **Beasts of India (2003)**

Bhajju Shyam would like to dedicate this book
to the memory of Jangarh Singh Shyam

Kodai Matsuoka would like to thank Akio Sugimoto and Sakurako Abe
for their assistance with this project.

Tara Books would like to thank Kiyoko Matsuoka of Itabashi Museum, Tokyo,
as well as Daisuke Kusakari and Mika Okubo of Bluesheep, Tokyo, for the exhibition
of our work in Japan in 2017 — an occasion which inspired this book.

We are grateful to the Pardhan Gond artists we have worked with for permission
to reproduce their work in this book. Thanks also to all our friends and their
families in Patangarh for extending their warm support to this project.

Origins of Art: The Gond Village of Patangarh

Kodai Matsuoka's text, translated from
the Japanese by Natsuko Nose

Bhajju Shyam's text, translated from
the Hindi by Shruti Buddhavarapu

Copyright © 2019 Tara Books Private Limited

For the text: Kodai Matsuoka and Bhajju Shyam

For the photographs: Kodai Matsuoka

For the illustrations: Various artists

Design: Ragini Siruguri

Editor: Natsuko Nose (for the Japanese text)

Silkscreened pages printed at AMM Screens, Chennai

For this edition:
Tara Publishing Ltd., UK <www.tarabooks.com/uk>
and
Tara Books Pvt. Ltd., India <www.tarabooks.com>

Production: C. Arumugam

Printed in India by Canara Traders and Printers, Pvt. Ltd.

All rights reserved. No part of this work may be reproduced in
any form without the prior written permission of the publisher.

ISBN: 978-81-939841-3-0